CÉSAR CHÁVEZ
Labor Leader

Written by Clara Sánchez de Morris
Illustrated by Richard Leonard

MODERN CURRICULUM PRESS

Program Reviewers

MODERN CURRICULUM PRESS

13900 Prospect Road, Cleveland, Ohio 44136

A Paramount Publishing Company

Copyright © 1994 Modern Curriculum Press, Inc.

ISBN 0-8136-5266-9 (Reinforced Binding)   0-8136-5272-3 (Paperback)

Library of Congress Catalog Card Number: 93-79440

Dear Readers,

This is the story of César Chávez, the leader of the United Farm Workers of America. All the members of his family were migrant farm workers. They had to work long, hard days.

As César grew up, he began to think of ways to make life better for migrant workers. Because he would not give up, he brought about many improvements for these workers. He stood up for what he believed in and helped many people.

Your friend,

Clara A S Morrie

A small desert farm near Yuma, Arizona, was the first home of César Chávez. Born in 1927, César grew up hearing stories from his grandfather about Mexico. He heard how his grandfather had come to the United States looking for a better life.

César was the second of six children
born to Librado and Juana Chávez.
Librado owned the farm and a store,
and was the local postmaster. From
his father, César learned it was
important to work hard.

In 1937, when César was only ten, his father had to sell the store and the farm. Times were hard. To find work, his parents moved their family from Arizona to California.

4

In California, the Chávez family became migrant workers. Migrant workers move from farm to farm picking fruits and vegetables for the owners.

César's family lived in migrant worker camps built by the land owners. The cabin rooms were small and bare. Often they did not have bathrooms, electricity, or water.

The whole Chávez family had to work in the fields. César and his brothers and sisters worked after school, on weekends, and every day during the summer. All of them worked very hard.

Because his family was always moving, César went to many different schools. He stopped going to school after the eighth grade. He had to spend his days working.

As he worked, César saw
something that made him very
angry. Many farm owners were
not fair to the migrant workers.
They did not pay the workers
enough for their long hours in
the fields.

César also thought the land
owners should give the
workers better places to live.

9

10

César decided he had to do
something . He began to talk with
other workers to find a way to make
things better. Some workers were
afraid to talk to César. They thought if
they complained to the land owners,
the workers might lose their jobs.

In 1944, World War II was going on. César joined the U.S. Navy. After the war was over, he returned to California and married Helen Fabela.

César and Helen became migrant workers on the big farms. At night, César began teaching others to read and write. More and more people came to know him and listen to what he had to say.

14

César helped the migrant workers start a union, a special kind of group. As a group, they could make the land owners listen to them. During the day César picked fruit. At night he talked to workers. He told them they should go to classes to become citizens of the United States.

César told them that together they could win more rights for themselves and their families. Many farm workers were afraid to join him. But César did not give up.

In 1962, César worked full time for his growing union. After six months there were over 300 members. He called his union the National Farm Workers Association (NFWA). Later it became the United Farm Workers (UFW).

In 1965, members of César's union began a strike against California grape growers. The workers left the fields. They would not pick the grapes until they received better pay and better places to live. The grapes began to rot.

17

18

19

NO GRAPES FOR SALE HERE

For over five years their strike went on. The grape growers brought in new workers to pick the grapes.

People from all over the country helped the strikers with food, clothes, and money. Some would not even buy or sell grapes. Finally the grape growers had to give in.

In 1970, the strike ended. The union had won! The workers would have more rights and better pay.

23

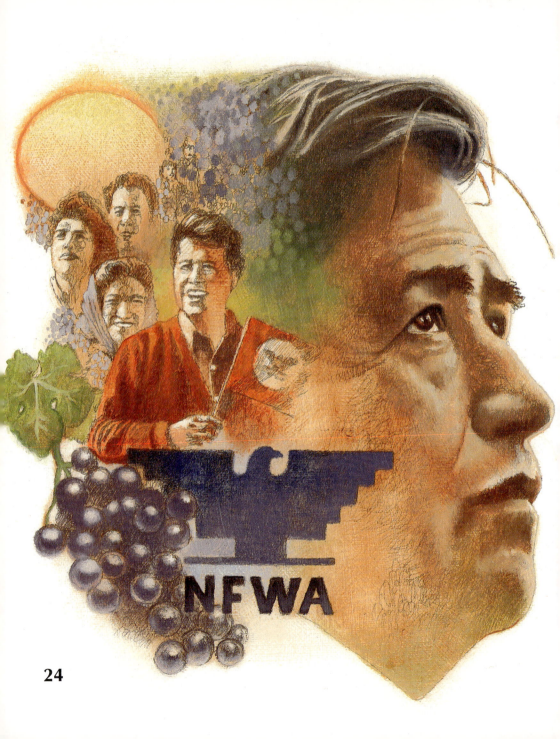

24

Until his death in 1993, César continued to work for the rights of farm workers. The Chávez children—Paul, Ana, Anthony, Fernando, Eloise, Sylvia, and Linda—all worked with him. They are proud of their father. From César they have learned to work hard and never give up.

Glossary

migrant (mī′ grənt) One who moves from
  one region to another regularly

organize (ôr′ gə nīz) To start and put into
  order

postmaster (pōst′ mas′ tər) A person in
  charge of the post office

strike (strīk) A demonstration in which employees
  stop working in order to get an employer to
  improve working conditions

union (yoon′ yən) A group of workers joined
  together to protect their interests

About the Author

Clara Sánchez de Morris is an administrator in the Second Language Programs Department in Las Vegas, Nevada. Mrs. Morris was born and raised in Mexico City, Mexico, and came to live in the United States in 1975. Her first teaching assignment here involved migrant students in Idaho. She feels that it is important for all students to become aware of the work and accomplishments of people who have dedicated their lives to make ours better. Mrs. Morris is also an interpreter/translator in English and Spanish. She dedicates this book to the memory of a dear friend, Uly Ramsey.

About the Illustrator

Born in Florida of Cuban heritage, Richard Leonard is a graduate of Pratt Institute in Brooklyn, New York. He has worked as an art director, illustrator of movie posters, and teacher, and now does freelance illustration, primarily commercial. He has also produced murals, book illustrations, and several works in galleries. His illustrations for *César Chávez* were created in oil on canvas, capturing the vibrance of the subject's life.